How To Get Rich

A Proven, Step By Step Guide For How To Make More Money, Getting Rich And Mastering The Game Of Money

Table Of Contents

Thank you! _____ 3

Introduction _____ 4

Chapter 1 – The Things Rich People Do _____ 6

Chapter 2 – How Mindset Can Set Up Everything _____ 8

Chapter 3 – Firstly, Get Out Of Debt _____ 10

Chapter 4 – Choose Which Asset Class Suits You _____ 13

Chapter 5 – Aspire – Acquire – Apply (Triple A Triangle) _ 15

Chapter 6 – The Game Of Money _____ 17

Chapter 7 – Money Tips _____ 19

Conclusion _____ 22

Check Out My Other Books _____ 24

Greetings from the Lean Stone Publishing Company _____ 25

Thank you!

I would like to thank you for buying this book!

If you like the book and get some value out of it, after reading it, I would appreciate if you could leave a positive review on the Amazon Kindle store.

Thank you and enjoy the book!

***

Receive e-mail updates on new book releases and free book promotions from Robert Gardner by signing up to the e-mail list: **http://bit.ly/list_robertgardner_cs**

***

Follow us, **Lean Stone Publishing**, the publishing company that published this book. You will receive e-mail information on upcoming book launches, free book promotions and much more. Sign up to this e-mail list: **http://bit.ly/list_lsp_cs**

***

Like us at **www.facebook.com/leanstonepublishing**

Follow us on Twitter **@leanstonebooks**

Introduction

Name a person who doesn't want to be rich. Silly question, isn't it? There's no person in this world who doesn't want to be rich. Some wanted to be rich in love, because it is a wonderful feeling. Others want to be rich in achievements, because the world is ought to know about their talents. But most people want to be rich with money. Nobody can blame them. Living today is not as easy as living before. Life hundreds of years ago was simple; it didn't have the luxury of technology and modernizations. Nowadays, however you need things not as a form of entertainment, you need them because they are necessary.

Is getting rich an easy goal? Well, for some, it may not even be a goal. There are people who are born naturally rich. Through their parents' efforts, they can eat sumptuous food anytime they want, go somewhere whenever they please, and buy anything when they want to. Others, on the other hand, became rich because of pure luck. They simply bought a lottery ticket and hours later, they become millionaires. Either way, they are lucky. If you are not included in the given scenarios, you still have the opportunity to become rich. You just need to work hard.

Working hard, being patient and being full of determination is perhaps the most fulfilling way of becoming rich. You will have the satisfaction of knowing that all your efforts and education have paid off. You will treasure every cent you have acquired because you worked hard to get them. It may have been a slow and rough journey, but you managed to become successful in the end.

This book will teach you how to become rich slowly. The following will be discussed:

- What are the things that rich people do differently? Can not-so rich people also do those things?

- How can mindset affect your goals in becoming rich?
- A method that can surely get you out of debts—and it's very easy to do!
- What are asset classes? What are the types of asset classes? How can you know what asset class suits you?
- What is the Triple A Triangle and how can it help you in your journey to become rich.
- What is the game of money and what strategies can you employ?

Now that you have the general idea, you can go ahead and turn to the next page. Be patient with the methods included in the book, but most importantly, be brave. You may feel a little disheartened, and that's normal, just keep in mind the teachings in this book and you'll surely go a long way.

Chapter 1 – The Things Rich People Do

Is there a thin line between rich and not-so rich people? Some of you will blame it on fate; others will think that disposition is the culprit. Well, the others are right. The difference between rich people and poor people are not so big in reality, but they become virtually huge because of disposition. Most people are not born rich, yes others were, but not all. Did you ever wonder how come a previous, self-supporting employee before became the boss that supports his own employees now? Perhaps he's doing things differently.

Here are some things that rich people do differently:

1. **They have GOALS** – Rich people put their goals in perspective. They know what they want and they want it to be solid, so they put it into writing. That way, they can focus on their objectives. Remembers that goals are not aspirations—they are not wishes that you want to have. They are things that you have to do. A wish goes like this: "I want to be rich." While a goal is something like: "I'll save 30% of my monthly income so I can start a small business after one year." See the difference?
2. **They WANT to improve** – Rich people have time for leisure, contrary to popular belief that they don't. In fact, they often read and watch TV. The difference is that they watch reality shows where they can learn something, and they read books that will help them improve. So much like what you are doing right now, you're reading a book that will help you become rich.
3. **They go the EXTRA mile** – Rich people do not settle for less. In fact, they are not even satisfied with "a good job". When they feel like they can still do something to make the work extraordinarily great, they will not

hesitate to do it. Mediocrity is not their game. How do you think they will become promoted in their job if all they do are average outputs? Their business will not flourish if they will be contented with "enough". Rich people go the extra mile.

4. ***They are NOT lucky*** – No, they do not frequently play the lottery to win the jackpot. And they don't dwell on luck to be rich. In fact, most of the rich people will be offended when someone tells them they are lucky. Why? Because they have worked hard to be where they are. It will be unfair to incorporate luck when they have been doing their job in the best of their abilities.

5. ***They are HEALTHY*** – Most rich people value their health like it is their lifeline, because in reality, it really is. They watch their diet and they do regular exercise since they know that no job can be accomplished if they are sick and bedridden.

Another thing, rich people do is smile. They know that they are doing the right thing so they feel very positive about themselves. If you want to be rich, you better start taking note of all these things. You don't need to change drastically, little by little will do.

Chapter 2 – How Mindset Can Set Up Everything

The thing is you want to be rich. You really want to, but your will just is not enough. Did you ever experience a situation where you came out victorious even when the world is out to get you? For example, you really want to attend the party but you have to finish a project and you even have an exam. You think of asking your friends or family for help and even bribed them with something to help you finish the project. Then you cram your studying. In the end you did it. Why? It is because you had the right motivation.

Being rich is not easy. But when you know what you'll get when you become rich, you'll start to have a positive mindset and a stronger will. In the light of that, let's have a look at what you can have and what you can do when you become rich:

1. ***Go anywhere you want*** – travel all you like because you have the money to spend. Just imagine yourself seeing some place in the TV or in the magazine and then decide that perhaps, next month you can arrange to travel there. Meet new people, experience new culture and eat delicacies. Never be a stranger to a distant family member because you will be able to visit them when you want to. If you want this kind of lifestyle, motivate yourself to become rich.
2. ***Buy the things you like*** – and you can buy them without the fear of looking at the price tag. It may sound a little materialistic for your liking, but who doesn't want the ability to go out in the mall and actually being able to like something that you like?
3. ***Provide for your loved ones*** – On a more personal level, being rich means being able to give your loved

ones not just what they need, but also what they like. No more self-pitying that you do not have the money to spend. This is perhaps the greatest motivation you can think of. Become rich and be the best provider for your family.

4. ***Helping others*** - When catastrophe strikes, you'll see people donating and doing something for the less fortunate. If you are rich, you can help big time. That's not to say though that when you are not rich, you won't be able to help. You still can, on your own ways. Remember that helping comes naturally to people. Surely you have talked to yourself at least once about "If only I have the money, I'll help that person."

5. ***Enjoying life*** – being rich means you'll be able to live with less worry. You won't be scared of the bills that will arrive at your doorstep. You won't fret when someone in your family becomes sick. You'll be able to enjoy waking up each day knowing that you and your loved ones are secured. There will be less stress, tension, and pressure.

Even when the world is against you, when you have the right motivation and the positive mindset, no one can ruin your game. Of course being rich is a long process, but it doesn't mean that it is completely impossible. Patience, effort and determination will take you there, so always have them along with your reason to be rich.

Chapter 3 – Firstly, Get Out Of Debt

Nobody gets rich when he or she has a lot of debt to pay. Frankly this is one of the reasons why people get discouraged of becoming rich and working hard. They will think that all the money they will be warning will just be put to paying all their debt. The truth is, you have to turn your debt into some form of a motivation! AFTER you have paid off everything, you will finally be free and then you can start planning on how to be rich.

Aside from the common constituents of paying off debt like determination and patience, you can also employ methods. This chapter will discuss the Debt Snow Ball Method: a surefire way of getting out of debt.

Instructions:

1. What you will have to do first is to list down all your debts. Don't be discouraged when you see a long list, it is okay. After doing that, arrange them from the lowest to highest amount. Don't bother with the interest; just think of the total amount and the payment per month.

   For example:

   Credit Card 1 Debt - $600 with a monthly payment of $50 and 10% interest

   Credit Card 2 Debt - $7200 with a monthly payment of $300 and 25% interest

   Credit Card 3 Debt - $10000 with a monthly payment of $500 and 5% interest

   We will just list down 3 debts. The examples are only for you to get the complete grasp of how Snowball Method works to pay off debt.

2. Budget your money. You have to be very restrictive. How much of your monthly income will be left and how much of it can be used to pay of your debt. In this example, let's say that you will have $1000 to use to pay for the debt.

   Let's take all the minimum payments:

   CC 1 - $50

   CC 2 - $300

   CC 3 - $500

   The total is $850. If you less that amount to $1000, there will still be $150 left.

3. Take that $150 and add it to the minimum payment of the lowest debt, which is CC 1. To make it simple, you'll be paying the following:

   CC 1 - $50 (Original) = $150 (Excess) = **$200**

   CC 2 - **$300**

   CC 3 - **$500**

   Just do this every month and after 3 months, you can proudly say that your Credit Card 1 Debt is completely paid off.

4. After you have paid off the smallest debt, take what you were originally paying for it and pay the second largest debt which is CC 2.

   Your payment will look like this:

   CC 1 – **CLEARED**

   CC 2 - $200 (from CC1 before) + $300 (Original) = **$500**

CC 3 - **$500**

After less than 13 months (12.6) you will be able to clear the second largest debt.

5. After paying off the two smallest debts, now put all the $500 in the largest debt.

    CC 1 – **CLEARED**

    CC 2 – **CLEARED**

    CC 3 - $500 (Original) + $500 (from CC2 before) = **$1000**

    After doing this for yet 2 another months, you'll be free of all your debts!

Chapter 4 – Choose Which Asset Class Suits You

Asset Class are group of securities that exhibit the same financial characteristics, have almost the same movements in the marketplace, and are under the same rules, laws, and regulations.

If you want to be rich, you have to consider which asset class will suit you best. In this chapter, several class assets will be discussed, you can use these information to decide the kind that you think will make you rich. Some of them may be more promising than the others, but it doesn't automatically mean that the less promising ones have less potential.

You have to make a thorough reflection within yourself before you can decide which asset class is for you.

1. **Paper Assets** – Basically paper assets consist of cash, stocks, bonds, mutual funds and such. In simpler terms, these are wealth *that usually can be converted easily to cash*. Paper assets monetary value is computed by taking all the investments of one person and converting it to how much he can sell it for. Investing in paper assets may require a great deal of knowledge, you can't just dive in with all your hard-earned money just because the stocks may seem popular or you know the company or brand. Knowing the ups and down of the economy as famous author and entrepreneur Robert Kiyosaki says, will help you if you want to be paper wealthy.
2. **Commodities** – Commodities are materials that are found on earth—good examples are crops, wheat, coffee, and the likes. Since they are commonly needed

in everyday living, they are easier to sell, ***thus easily converted to cash***. Unlike paper assets that need to wait and undergo several proceedings, commodities should be sold quickly because they are often perishable. Commodities ***are also subject to disasters*** such as typhoons. So if you are a farmer and you think that a typhoon can ruin your crops, you will harvest everything salvageable and sell it to a higher price because the farm is damaged.

3. ***Business*** – Is perhaps the most commonly preferred asset class. It gives you the freedom to choose what type, and how big your asset will become. You can sell items or services depending on your expertise and of course, your capital. Money coming from the businesses are easy often times easier to liquidate—thus, letting you know right away if you are losing or gaining cash. People who want to get rich often start with this type of asset because ***it can be started small.***

4. ***Real Estate*** – are lots, buildings, houses, resorts, along with the commodities that come from it. If for example you have purchased a land and it was found to have precious metals, you also own the precious metals, and it will make the value of your asset higher. Turning into real estate asset is a huge step and would often require huge capital. If you do not have the properties to sell, you can opt to be a real estate broker—one that sells someone else's property. For an instance, if the owner wants his property to be sold at the price of $550,000 you can earn money by a) earning a commission (the owner will declare how many percent) and b) by putting your own price on top (if you sold it at $600, 000, the $50,000 is yours.)

Remember to choose carefully. Take everything into consideration: the current money you have, the time you can spend, and your interest. All these will play a role in making you richer slowly.

Chapter 5 – Aspire – Acquire – Apply (Triple A Triangle)

The Triple A Triangle is not something that can get you rich tomorrow. After all, this book is about becoming rich one step at a time. Triple A Triangle is a system that anyone can use. In fact, it is something that everyone should use. It considers the mindset and goals of an individual—which are the most important keys to getting rich. The Triple A Triangle will keep you on your toes, reminding you to be patient and always have the determination to pursue your dream, which is, to become rich.

- *Aspire* – This is the "dreaming" part of the triangle. In this instance, you want to be rich. You want to be a millionaire. Does it stop there? No. Think of the things that you will have once you have ACCOMPLISHED your dream. Look back on the goals that you have written. You'll be able to continue with your love of travel, you'll be able to send your kids to great school, you'll be able to donate a huge sum of money to your favorite charity organization. When you have something to gain, you'll aspire more solidly. So, start with aspirations. Aspire to be rich.
- *Acquire* – This is the "learning" part of the triangle. Before you become rich, you have to educate yourself first. This part will take time. You cannot learn everything overnight. You can read books, watch television or even interview and talk to people that inspires you. Aside from educating yourself, you also have to continue building your determination and bravery. From time to time, think about your aspirations. Don't let them go. If you feel like there's

just too much to do, tell yourself that it's because there's also a lot to gain. Be patient, and determined.
- *Apply* – Is the most difficult part of the triangle. This is also the "doing" part. Most people will stop right here because they fear that they will fail miserably. Application is the step that will take you there. What was the use of having the aspirations and the education if you will not do something concrete about them? Like the previous step, you have to continuously think about your goals. Then think about everything that you have learned. Then apply them to what you have in mind.

The three major focus of the triangle is all about trusting yourself and believing that something good will come out with your goals and education. Actions are necessary; after all, you cannot get rich with just dreaming and learning. Be patient, in the first part of the application process, you might experience failure, but it doesn't mean that you have learned nothing. Don't be too hard on yourself and try until you get the hang of it.

Chapter 6 – The Game Of Money

After aspiring, acquiring and applying, you have to gain mastery. Consider getting rich a game. Your money is the score card, but what's at stake are your aspirations and education. If you lose the game, you lose your goals: no more travelling, no more awesome school for kids, and no more donating to your favorite charity. What's even worse is you'll have to admit that everything you have learned will be wasted.

Don't worry though, like any other game, you will have strategies you can use. You may lose small things, or lose big time, but the game doesn't end until you give up. So the number one rule is to not give up—if you do, game's over.

1. Place your bet – carefully think about how much you are willing to invest. Most people will use sleeping money- one that they don't really need. Others are brave enough to risk valuable cash. Whatever money you choose to invest, think about the pros and the cons carefully. It is highly recommended to "earn" first before placing bets. That way, whatever happens, you won't lose the money for tuition or the money for mortgage.
2. Play it well – planning is not an option, it is a must. A beginner must not be greedy. Remember, you are building your reputation; you have to build it well. This step will focus more on your assets. If you have a business, make sure your products and services are of high quality. Don't forget about promotion and marketing strategies. Make sure you offer superb customer support and assistance. If the profits are not promising, that's okay. You're just on the first leg so a

little progress is expected and you should reward yourself for that.
3. Look for competitors and predators – Competition is good, but predation is not. If your business has an opponent that's too big for you to handle, it will be best to lay low. Wait for your right time and think of other things that can set you apart from the tycoons. Be confident. Just because you're starting out small doesn't mean you have no hopes at all. Competitors are also great motivators; you can learn great deal of knowledge from them.
4. Be patient – Failure means another opportunity to improve. Be patient. Don't stop just because something went wrong. Remember that the game is at your disposal: it will end when you give up.
5. Manage your score cards – congratulate yourself for small achievements. For a starter, that's great! The money you have earned can be used to fulfill one of your small goals. If not, you can save it for the mean time. Don't stop with small winnings- continue to strive and be successful.

The game can be considered a gamble, so always be on the lookout. Watch your score cards and add more winnings.

Chapter 7 – Money Tips

Money is a necessity. You generally can't go about your day without using any. I know that you have learned various techniques on how you can get rich slowly with this book, but even if you stick to everything you have learned here, but then splurge all of your money the minute you get your hands on it, then unfortunately, you won't be able to stay rich for long.

In line with that, I have listed different tips and strategies that you can try in order to save your hard-earned money.

On Food

1. If you can bring packed lunch to your office, then do so. The few dollars that you will be able to save per meal will be a great addition to your savings, not only will eating packed lunch save you money but is also healthier.

2. Never go grocery shopping when you're hungry. You might not notice it, but when you do so, your brain always signals you to buy something you think you need, when in fact you only want to buy it because you are hungry and you want to eat that now.

3. Say goodbye to eating out, instead stay at home and prepare something that is special to you and your family. In this way you can get to bond with them while being able to save.

On Buying

1. When in a grocery, practice the 30 second rule. When you are having second thought in buying something, or just before you place a food in your cart, return it to the shelf and continue shopping. Before you leave that aisle, look back at that item, if you still want to buy the item you returned to the shelf then go get it back.

2. In the same light as the rule above, a 30-day rule exists for wanting to buy something expensive. If you are about to swipe you credit card for something expensive that you have "convinced" yourself that you really need, stop first and go home. Wait for 30 days to pass by, after 30 days assess if you still want that item, chances are, you don't. But if you still do, then go ahead and buy it.

3. When you go shopping, don't buy anything just because you like an item. Consider some things before you fall in line in the cashier. Will you be using that item today, tomorrow or in the next week? Are you going to be able to use it at least once or twice a week? If no, then don't buy it. If yes, then buy it.

On Enjoying

1. During the weekend, it is not necessary to go out and treat your children in expensive theme parks or malls. One option is to invest in board games or family games that you can play at home during the weekends. You can also buy a portable pool or a trampoline that you can use in your backyard. In this way, your kids will enjoy while you are able to save.

2. Instead of purchasing books, you can borrow them from friend and just return it after you have read it. You can also choose to buy e-books instead. In this way you will be able to save while you are keeping clutters from your home.

3. If you have a collection, no matter what it is, try to lessen the number that you acquire within a year or month. For example, if you are collecting bags, and you are used to buying different kinds of expensive bags every month, then try to lessen it to every other month instead.

On Your Social Side

1. Keep a list of your loved ones' birthdays, anniversaries and special days. Plan in advance what thoughtful gift you can give them. Make it a point to add more personal touches to your gifts. Not only will it be sweeter and more special, but it is also cheaper to buy and make.

2. During special occasions, consider putting up a potluck party instead of going out on a fancy restaurant. This will save you time and money and it will also be a more personal event when it is done in your home.

3. Every Christmas, discuss with your family a gift giving limit for everyone. This mean that there will be a certain amount that cannot be reached when buying gifts for your family member. If your kids gets used to this rule, not only will you be able to save, but you will also be able to teach your kids the value of money.

There you go, these are just some tips that you can consider in order to be able to save money. Getting rich is not a walk in the park. For some, it might be a leap of fate, or they were born rich, but for some, they have to work hard for it. So if you are one of those people who have to work hard to be rich, then I would like to bid you good luck, and embody these so that you will be able to save money from what you will earn while trying to win in the game of life. Remember that all your hard work will be for naught if you don't take care of your money, stop splurging and start spending wisely.

***

Receive e-mail updates on new book releases and free book promotions from Robert Gardner. By visiting the link below
http://bit.ly/list_robertgardner_cs

***

Conclusion

Have you taken a deep breath? If you still haven't, you can do so now. You did a really great job in finishing this book from cover to cover. However, it's just the beginning. You won't get rich by just finishing a book, you have to act. Remember the "application" part in the Triple A Triangle? That part is very important. Don't be scared to start. One good way of obtaining bravery is building your foundations well—that means your goals, education, patience and determination.

Let's make a wick recap of what you have learned in this book:

- The things that rich people do differently and the knowledge that you too can do them.
- Positivity is the key, don't let it go.
- A surefire way of getting out of debt.
- Class assets and the manner of choosing what can suit you.
- The Triple A Triangle
- The Game of Money

Now that you have all those knowledge, you have to be reminded of several things:

- Never forget about your family – in your quest to become rich, never forget about your loved ones. Remember that they are included in your goals. If you will forget them, what is the good in getting rich? Don't miss an opportunity to be with them, after all, money alone cannot keep you happy.
- Never take your health for granted – health is wealth. Keep that in mind. What's the use of money when you will only spend it on medications, medical procedures,

or surgery? Eat healthy foods, rest when needed, don't forget to exercise. You need all the strength to venture on your success.

- Sleep with a good conscience – Don't be greedy. Being blind of your morals and dignity will take you nowhere. Where can your money take you when you have enemies all around? Play well, but don't forget to play fair. Having a peace of mind is perhaps the greatest non-material wealth you'll have. Why forsake it paper bills that cannot buy you a contented, happy heart?

Being rich is great. There's no denying in that fact. The designer's clothes and expensive jewelry, all of them can make you happy—but only for a while. So work hard on getting rich, but always maintain a good heart. Golden intentions will keep you happy, and it can take you to great heights.

What will you do next? Set up your goals! List them all down to make them more concrete. And then, educate yourself. Learn from books, TV shows, but most importantly, learn from people. Lastly, apply what you have learned.

Do your best and you will succeed!

***

Receive e-mail updates on new book releases and free book promotions from Robert Gardner. By visiting the link below
http://bit.ly/list_robertgardner_cs

***

Check Out My Other Books

You will find these books by simply searching for them on Amazon.com

Imagine never having to wake up to an alarm clock ever again. Never having to ask for permission for time off. Doing work you not only love, but work that pays you even when you are off traveling.

Broken into three sections, this book gives you immediate solutions to your money needs as well as specific guidance on how to make money online and more advanced options once you have started make some fast money.

Greetings from the Lean Stone Publishing Company

We want to thank you so much for reading this book to the end. We are committed to creating life changing books in the Self Help area, such as this one that you just read.

If you liked this book and want to follow us for more information on upcoming book launches, free promotions and special offers, then follow us on Facebook and Twitter!

Sign up for e-mail updates on new releases and free promotions by visiting this link:

http://bit.ly/list_lsp_cs

Like us: **www.facebook.com/leanstonepublishing**

Follow: **@leanstonebooks**

Thank you again for reading to the end, it means the world to us!

Printed in Great Britain
by Amazon